Eimar O'Duffy

THE IRISH WRITERS SERIES

James F. Carens, General Editor

TITLE	*AUTHOR*
SEAN O'CASEY	Bernard Benstock
J. C. MANGAN	James Kilroy
W. R. RODGERS	Darcy O'Brien
STANDISH O'GRADY	Phillip L. Marcus
PAUL VINCENT CARROLL	Paul A. Doyle
SEUMAS O'KELLY	George Brandon Saul
SHERIDAN LEFANU	Michael Begnal
AUSTIN CLARKE	John Jordan
BRIAN FRIEL	D. E. S. Maxwell
DANIEL CORKERY	George Brandon Saul
EIMAR O'DUFFY	Robert Hogan
MERVYN WALL	Robert Hogan
FRANK O'CONNOR	James Matthews
GEORGE MOORE	Janet Egleson
JAMES JOYCE	Fritz Senn
JOHN BUTLER YEATS	Douglas Archibald
LORD EDWARD DUNSANY	Zack Bowen
MARIA EDGEWORTH	James Newcomer
MARY LAVIN	Zack Bowen
OSCAR WILDE	Edward Partridge
SOMERVILLE AND ROSS	John Cronin
SUSAN L. MITCHELL	Richard M. Kain
J. M. SYNGE	Robin Skelton
KATHARINE TYNAN	Marilyn Gaddis Rose
LIAM O'FLAHERTY	James O'Brien
IRIS MURDOCH	Donna Gerstenberger
JAMES STEPHENS	Brigit Bramsback
BENEDICT KIELY	Daniel Casey
EDWARD MARTYN	Robert Christopher
BRENDAN BEHAN	John Stewart Collis
DOUGLAS HYDE	Gareth Dunleavy
EDNA O'BRIEN	Grace Eckley
CHARLES LEVER	M. S. Elliott
BRIAN MOORE	Jeanne Flood
SAMUEL BECKETT	Clive Hart
ELIZABETH BOWEN	Edwin J. Kenney
JOHN MONTAGUE	Frank Kersnowski
ROBERT MATURIN	Robert E. Lougy
GEORGE FITZMAURICE	Arthur E. McGuinness
MICHAEL MCCLAVERTY	Leo F. McNamara
FRANCIS STUART	J. H. Natterstad
PATRICK KAVANAGH	Darcy O'Brien
BRINSLEY MACNAMARA AND GEORGE SHIELS	Raymond J. Porter
STEPHEN MACKENNA	Roger Rosenblatt
JACK B. YEATS	Robin Skelton
WILLIAM ALLINGHAM	Alan Warner
SAMUEL LOVER	Mabel Worthington
FLANN O'BRIEN	Bernard Benstock
DENIS JOHNSTON	James F. Carens
WILLIAM LARMINIE	Richard J. Finneran

EIMAR O'DUFFY

Robert Hogan

Lewisburg
BUCKNELL UNIVERSITY PRESS

Associated University Presses, Inc.
Cranbury, New Jersey 08512

Library of Congress Cataloging in Publication Data

Hogan, Robert Goode, 1930–
Eimar O'Duffy.
(The Irish writers series)
Bibliography: p.
1. O'Duffy, Eimar, 1893–1935.
PR6029.D76Z8 828'.9'1209 70–125469
ISBN 0-8387-7755-4
ISBN 0-8387-7665-5 (pbk.)

Printed in the United States of America

Contents

Acknowledgments	7
Chronology	9
I	13
II	28
III	51
IV	66
Bibliography	82

Acknowledgments

Grateful acknowledgment is made to Macmillan Services, Ltd., for permission to quote from *The Wasted Island, King Goshawk and the Birds* and *The Spacious Adventures of the Man in the Street;* to G. P. Putnam's Sons for permission to quote from *Asses in Clover* and *Love and Money;* and to the Society of Authors for permission to quote from Bernard Shaw's *Everybody's Political What's What.* I must also thank the University of Delaware for a summer fellowship to work on this book, Mr. Mervyn Wall and Mr. Conor Cruise O'Brien for answering various queries, and especially Mrs. Eimar O'Duffy for her graciousness, helpfulness and time.

R. H.

Chronology

1893	Born September 29, in Dublin, eldest son of Kevin O'Duffy, prominent surgeon dentist.
1903–1913	Attends school in England; graduates from University College, Dublin, with a Bachelor of Dental Surgery degree; becomes a member of the Irish Republican Brotherhood.
1913–1916	Prominent in the Irish Volunteers; has two plays presented by Edward Martyn's Irish Theatre.
1919	Publishes first novel, *The Wasted Island.*
1920	Marries, August 16, Kathleen Cruise O'Brien.
1921	Son Brian born on August 23.
1922	Publishes *Printer's Errors* and *The Lion and the Fox.*
1923	Publishes *Miss Rudd and Some Lovers.*
1924	Daughter Rosalind born on September 14.
1925	Moves to England, then free-lances in Paris and works for an American newspaper.
1926	Publishes *King Goshawk and the Birds.*

1928	Publishes *The Spacious Adventures of the Man in the Street.*
1929	Publishes revised version of *The Wasted Island.*
1932–1935	Publishes *Life and Money,* various mystery novels, *Asses in Clover;* dies in Surrey.

Eimar O'Duffy

I

Eimar Ultan O'Duffy is virtually a forgotten writer. In 1946, eleven years after his death, Vivian Mercier wrote an appreciative essay on his work in *The Bell,* and that essay is the only critical comment of any length on O'Duffy which I have been able to discover. In it, Mercier remarked:

> The late Eimar O'Duffy, modern Ireland's only prose satirist, was neither hanged nor drowned; he was simply ignored. Since his premature death in 1935 of duodenal ulcers—a satirist's occupational disease—what reputation he had has dwindled away to almost nothing. A few people still read his long, bitter, ill-written novel about 1916 and the events leading up to it, *The Wasted Island;* his masterpiece, the satire entitled *King Goshawk and the Birds,* has a few devotees who re-read it for the vigour of its headlong assault upon our whole modern civilization; apart from these two books, however, O'Duffy's work is unknown outside a small circle of friends and 'fans.'

In the 25 years since that was written, O'Duffy's reputation has, if anything, diminished even more. None of his books is in print, and the only critical discussion of his works in recent years has been a couple of pages in Benedict Kiely's *Modern Irish Fiction—A Critique* and a few more in Mercier's *The Irish Comic Tradition.*

O'Duffy was assuredly a writer of very uneven merit, and circumstances compelled him to try his hand at many genres—light verse, drama, light fiction, detective thrillers, the historical novel, the political novel, satire, and popular economics. A good deal of what he wrote is rather negligible, but his early novel *The Wasted Island* is a flawed near-masterpiece, and his satiric Cuandine trilogy, although it tapers off disastrously in its third book, is so fine in its first two books that one is driven to enthusiastic comparisons with Swift and Shaw.

O'Duffy was a child of his times. He was born in 1893, the oldest son of Kevin O'Duffy, a prominent Anglo-Irish dentist. He was himself trained as a dentist and received a Bachelor of Dental Surgery degree at the National University. However, he disliked dentistry and practiced for only a short time. He was a small man with handsome, finely-chiselled features. Although he could be a congenial companion, he could also be difficult. According to his wife, the aunt of the notable writer and politician Conor Cruise O'Brien, the reason for his occasional irascibility was that he was frequently in excruciating pain. This lifelong agony was the result of the ulcer trouble that he contracted early in the war years, and that was undoubtedly aggravated by a serious altercation with his father. The elder O'Duffy demanded that his son join the British army, and when the son refused the father expelled him from the family home.

The rift was made complete when young O'Duffy became involved in the Irish National movement. He became a captain in the Irish Volunteers and wrote frequently for its newspaper. In a typescript contained in the National Library of Ireland, Bulmer Hobson, who edited *The Irish Volunteer,* wrote of it:

> The two most valuable contributors were J. J. O'Connell, afterwards Col. O'Connell of the Irish Army, and Eimar O'Duffy, who won distinction as a playwright and novelist. The military articles in the paper were written by these two men. Both men had a great interest in, and a natural aptitude for military things. . . . O'Duffy's interest in the subject apparently started when he was a Cadet at Stoneyhurst.

Hobson also mentions that he suggested to O'Connell and O'Duffy "that, in writing for the paper, they should specialise in the development of guerilla tactics suitable to the Irish terrain. . . ." Most of the many military articles in the paper were unsigned, and so it is usually impossible to know what is by O'Duffy and what is by O'Connell. Some of the articles were training aids and hints, but there was also an interesting series of analyses of famous battles, and this I suspect to be O'Duffy's. His first signed article, however, was a short interview in 1915 with the widow of O'Donovan Rossa. In October, 1915, O'Duffy began a column called "A Military Causerie," a series characterized by commonsensical advice and exhortation. Some of the remarks affect a youthful callousness which O'Duffy a few years later would consider painfully naive. For instance, in an article which appeared on November 27, 1915, he wrote:

> What we really must cultivate is a frame of mind that will face the expenditure of cannon-fodder philosophically. Look at it this way. Before you question can you

> afford to win, ask yourself can you afford to be beaten. You know very well you can't. Therefore, you must win, whatever the price. If you consider the price of victory too high, don't fight.

Or, on December 4, 1915:

> When a nation in arms sets out on a definite task it sticks at nothing.... A nation when she is fighting has not time to weep. There is time enough afterwards. A nation when she is fighting cannot count the cost. The sacrifice of young lives is cruel, but it is necessary.

This is rather close to the views of Padraic Pearse who, according to Hobson and also to O'Duffy when he came to write *The Wasted Island,* "became convinced of the necessity for a periodic blood sacrifice to keep the National Spirit alive." It is a view which O'Duffy came to regard with repugnance.

The closest approach in "A Military Causerie" to literature is in three little satires written early in 1916. One called "Le Debacle" treats of an idealistic young Volunteer named Cornelius Cannon who spent his time studying great tomes about past battles and neglected small current details of discipline, drill, and commonsense. The second, "La Triomphe," is a remarkably fine piece of imaginative writing, which describes how Cornelius, now thoroughly reformed and practical, commands a losing action in the field. The third, "Poet and Hard Chaw," contrasts a Pearse-like second lieutenant with a practical soldier. Of the lieutenant, O'Duffy wrote:

> His friends called him an Idealist, a Poet; his enemies a Dreamer, a Versifier. This puts it rather broadly, but there were sub-groups under each heading. His bosom friends called him a great man; his worst enemies asserted

that he was an Ass. And yet again there were certain cynical people who merely said he was a good Nationalist but not much use either as a Poet or as a Lieutenant. This was strange, for I firmly believe that it was his poetry that got him his lieutenancy, and all the world knows that his lieutenancy inspired him to more poetry.

O'Duffy's own captaincy was not universally popular either. In Chapter IX of his manuscript *History of the Irish Volunteers* (contained in the National Library of Ireland), O'Duffy's colleague J. J. O'Connell made these remarks about the training of noncommissioned officers in the Dublin Brigade of the Volunteers:

> It happened that Capt. O'Duffy was unemployed at the moment and I urged that he was precisely the man for the task of training N. C. O.'s. I was somewhat surprised to find on the part of some members of the staff a very marked animus against Captain O'Duffy. His extreme youth—he was only twenty at the time—was urged against him. I mentioned that if his efficiency was admitted his age didn't matter. Another objection was his manner—"the manner of the O. T. C. [Officer's Training Corps for the British army]" as it was described. To this I answered that it does not do for an N. C. O. to be thin-skinned. If he is sensitive about what is said to himself, he will be too careful about what he says to his subordinates—and will inevitably be a dismal failure in consequence. As a matter of fact I believe that Capt. O'Duffy's abruptness had an excellent effect in sharpening the subordinate command of the Brigade.

All such preparations were to be of a much more immediate practicality than O'Duffy or some of his chiefs realized. As Hobson wrote in his memoir of the Rising:

> The first definite information I had that an insurrection was to occur in the immediate future was late in the evening of Holy Thursday, when J. J. O'Connell and Eimar O'Duffy came into my office and told me that an

> insurrection had been planned for the following Saturday. With them I went immediately to MacNeill's house in Rathfarnam, arriving a considerable time after he had gone to bed. We got MacNeill up and hastened then to St. Enda's to see P. H. Pearse, arriving about 2 A. M., then knocking Pearse up. MacNeill, O'Connell and I went in to see Pearse, leaving O'Duffy, who was not a member of the Executive, outside. Pearse then admitted that an insurrection was to take place, and told us that nothing we could do could prevent it.

O'Duffy was then sent by Eoin MacNeill, the nominal if not the practical head of the Volunteers, to Belfast in those crucial days immediately before the Rising, to quash any insurgency there.

O'Duffy's disillusionment with the Rising was rather like that of Sean O'Casey, and he withdrew from the Nationalist movement after the Rising and fell back upon his already deeply ingrained socialist principles. He did, however, stay in Ireland until 1925, when "embittered by his experience of the national movement and by losing his post in the Department of External Affairs," he moved to England. He was by this time married and supporting a family, but ill health, bad luck, and a succession of jobs left him little time to write at leisure and without worry. His most successful book, *King Goshawk and the Birds,* was much more a critical than a popular success, and he was driven to turn out potboiling detective thrillers. Except for them, his writing until his death was basically a criticism of the capitalistic system which had spectacularly broken down and caused the great Depression of the 1930s. When he died in 1935 after an operation, he was still a young man. His work, however, had failed to make any wide or lasting impact, and his death passed virtually unnoticed. Even P. S. O'Hegarty, in a short, appreciative obituary which appeared in *The Dublin Magazine* wrote that he died "before his talent had come to anything like full fruition."

O'Duffy was a facile writer, too facile, and his facility as well as his satiric bent is evident in the early light verse, which he collected in a slim volume published in 1918, *A Lay of the Liffey.* His verses are somewhat uneven, and none of them has any great merit. The following stanzas from the poem "Consolation," however, show the mildly Gilbertian ease that he was able to attain at his best.

Michael Macadam McCarthy McCann
Was a very myopic edentulous man,
And quite adipose.—In short he was fat
And toothless as well, and as blind as a bat.

The hair which had formerly grown from his head
Had grown right away and left nothing instead.
His auricular sense was nothing to boast.
In short he was bald and deaf as a post.

He was fed by injections; and never could tell
A Camembert cheese from a rose by the smell.
In short all his senses had gone to the wall,
So I think you'll agree he had no sense at all.

Probably the closest he came to a successful poem in the book is "The West Briton," a satiric view of the Anglo-Irish attitude during the World War:

I thank the goodness and the grace
That on my birth have smiled,
And made me in these Christian days,
A happy English child.

I thank the goodly god of Gold
Who has denied me naught,
Who has increased me fifty-fold
Because I have not thought.

I thank the god that gave the lie
To what the Saviour quoth,
And made it possible that I
Serve God and Mammon both.

I thank him yet again that he
Hath granted me this lot:

Two lands at war, yet I can be
In each a patriot.

I thank him too that I can love
My enemies so well
That I am sure of Heaven above
And have no fear of Hell.

And thee I thank, whoe'er thou art,
The god that gave me this:
That mine should be the pleasant part
A *mighty* foot to kiss.

He could occasionally rise to an effective comic rhyme, like "maybe I" and "Labii," and his metre usually canters effortlessly along, as in the title poem, which begins:

An original poem is hard to indite,
When all possible subjects are outré or trite.
On the one hand you're weary of poets who sing
Of war, or the skylark, or love, or the spring.
And yet, if I took the extravagant bent,
With an "Ode to a Lamprey" or "Hymn to Cement,"
I'm sure that you'd raise a unanimous shout:
"He's no poet at all! Shut him up! Put him out!"

"He's no poet at all! Shut him up! Put him out!" is

probably a fair judgment. None of his verses is without flat or thin spots. He was certainly more adroit than was Sean O'Casey who was writing poems at the same time, but O'Duffy's have no other merit than to illustrate that his fluency with words and his satiric bent were present from the very first.

O'Duffy's plays do retain considerable merit. Two of them were produced. Edward Martyn's Irish Theatre produced *The Phoenix on the Roof* at the Hardwicke Street theatre from January 4 to 9, 1915, and it was revived for a week's run on December 27. From April 19 to 24, the theatre presented O'Duffy's *The Walls of Athens* on a double bill with Thomas MacDonagh's *Pagans. The Phoenix on the Roof* has not been published, and I have not been able so far to find a record of the production of O'Duffy's other early play, *Bricriu's Feast,* or of his unpublished last play, *Malachy the Great.*

The Walls of Athens is nominally a play in three acts, but actually only a longish one-act. It is subtitled "A Comedy in Allegory," but is not really an allegory, and its comedy is more wry than comic. Set in Athens in 405 B.C., it tells in a mildly Shavian vein of the last days of the long war with Sparta. Despite the breezy modernity of the dialogue, the play would still seem a rather muted Shavian piece, for it lacks the plethora of jokes and paradoxes and free-wheeling rhetorical fireworks usually associated with GBS. Nevertheless, it is basically Shavian in its tone and attitude, and although quiet and minor it has lost little of its effect.

The main character is a pre-Brechtian version of Mother Courage, a vegetable seller named Mother Phrynne, who sells her wares against one of the two parallel walls that connect Athens with her seaport, Piraeus. Although Athens is in the final stages of starvation, Phrynne somehow contrives to have for her customers a bit of garlic or, at worst, a dead rat. She is not without kindness, for she does give a starving baby some milk, but her overriding concern is to keep the wall, where she has placed her stall for thirty years, standing. To accomplish her aim, she is thoroughly unscrupulous. She denounces an Athenian leader and blackmails a Spartan leader. And at the end of the play, when many brave and powerful men are either dead or disgraced, she remains with her stall before the bit of wall which she has managed to save. This is a much shorter play than *Mother Courage,* and of course much less powerful and moving. Nevertheless, the similarity is striking. Phrynne is much cannier, though, than Courage. Courage manages to hold on to a semblance of her old life by a dogged indomitability. Phrynne wins out by having a more realistic view of human nature than do the other people around her. "People," she says, "don't want to think they've been saved from themselves. They don't like to think they're being played with. If you want to rule them you must pretend to serve them; if you want to advise them, you must pretend to consult them. . . . There's never any need to climb higher than an apple-barrel."

This is a short, quiet play which does not aim high but does aim accurately. It is intelligent in conception and fluent in dialogue. If compared with some of the Abbey plays of this period—say, the popular pieces of

W. F. Casey and R. J. Ray, or those of A. Patrick Wilson, Martin J. McHugh, or J. Bernard MacCarthy—it comes off remarkably well. It could be staged today, as Casey and Ray distinctly could not, with little diminution of its original limited but telling effect.

Bricriu's Feast, published probably in 1919, is really a three-act play. It is a comedy, and its characters are Cuchullain, the Red Branch Knights, Queen Maeve, and others figures from the heroic sagas. Most of the humor of the play comes from O'Duffy's prosaic and realistic treatment of the characters, much in the way in which Shaw treated history in such plays as *Caesar and Cleopatra* and *Androcles and the Lion.* The tone is set immediately by the opening exchange between Bricriu and his wife:

Niabh: Bricriu!
Bricriu (*Inattentively*) : Um?

The traditional and expected aura of heroism is quickly punctured in such speeches as the following by the satiric hero, Bricriu:

> I know exactly what they'd do under all circumstances. I know how many gallons of blood they'd spill for this, and how many heads they'd strike off for that. They always tell me, whenever they get the chance. It's all very interesting and thrilling, and it amuses the ladies, but, once and for all, let me tell you that I will not have them held up to me as models. I decline to conform to any type, and to this one especially. . . . What you see in the lot of them I really can't understand. Take Celtchar, son of what's-his-name, for instance: What has he to talk about but his horses and his exploits?—and, such exploits! Then there's that bostboon, Laegaire, a dour, heavy warrior—not too successful, either—and always full of excuses for his defeats. Conal Cearnach isn't so bad, but his sense of humour is of the crudest. The best of them is that nice-looking boy, Cuchulain; but he's absurdly unsophisticated. . . .

Bricriu is the gadfly of the ancient Irish world, always stirring up argument and controversy. He invites the knights to a feast purposely to embroil them in a fight. This fight scene is amusingly developed in broad satiric style, with all of the heroes' wives becoming involved in it, with Cuchulain lifting up the corner of the house, and finally with Bricriu being hurled out of the window.

Bricriu stirs up controversy among the warriors, and Act II is largely devoted to a satirically handled poetic contest, in which O'Duffy satirizes the Irish literary penchant for romanticism and mysticism. Here he undoubtedly had in mind much of the work of the Celtic Twilight—the early work of Yeats, the work of AE, Seamus O'Sullivan, James Cousins, and others. The poems, however, which O'Duffy composes for his poets hover between parody and pastiche, and are hardly as cuttingly memorable as the subject undoubtedly deserves.

The third act is taken up with the Irish version of the Sir Gawain and the Green Knight story, in which the giant Curoi Mac Daire finds two of the heroes failing in courage, but in which Cuchulain, despite his fear, lays his head on the block. The giant then awards him the Sovereignty of the Heroes of Erin, and stalks off.

The plays falls into three distinct episodes, but each has a common meaning which is underlined in the short epilogue. There, Bricriu explains to Cuchulain:

> . . . I foresaw a danger to Ulster, lest she also should achieve contentment by falling under the spell of her own military glory. I feared that her heroes might rest and get fat by feasting and bragging, and her poets fall

> back on the deeds of the past for their themes. So I decided to be a centre of strife in the province, and to that object I have devoted my life.

The character of Bricriu was an important one for O'Duffy, and is alluded to in other, later works. O'Duffy, like Bricriu, was a satirist. If he did not, like Bricriu, become the conscience of his race, the reason was not that he did not try, but that he was defeated by circumstances which he could hardly control.

O'Duffy's misfortune as a playwright is that the conception and even the tone of his plays insist upon a comparison with Shaw, and O'Duffy's work emerges from that comparison looking rather bland and pale. Nevertheless, *Bricriu's Feast* is a longer, better play than *The Walls of Athens.* It is engaging, fluent, lively, and in the context of what was being written for the Irish stage in 1915 it is highly original. It was most distinctly not the kind of play likely to be done at the Abbey Theatre, whose treatment of the heroic material had always been —despite Standish O'Grady's opinion to the contrary— reverent. On the other hand, *Bricriu's Feast* was much better than many plays which the national theatre produced. Even more than *The Walls of Athens,* it would bear revival.

O'Duffy's most ambitious play is unpublished and, so far as I know, unproduced. Titled *Malachy the Great,* it was begun much later than those discussed above, in June 1928. It was finished in November 1930, and in 1933 it was submitted by P. S. O'Hegarty to the Dublin Gate Theatre, whose reading committee rejected it.

Set at the end of the tenth century, it is a five-act historical drama which treats the same material as does Lady Gregory's *Kincora.* But while Lady Gregory's drama constricted the scope of history almost to the size of a domestic wrangle, O'Duffy's is no less than Shakespearean in its conception. Its twelve scenes present a sprawling tale of intrigues, battles, alarums and excursions. Its cast has nineteen significant characters and the usual large assemblage of soldiers, attendants, dancers, and spear-carriers.

Kincora was not among Lady Gregory's best plays, but by narrowing her focus she avoided problems upon which O'Duffy's play founders. Chiefly, because of her less grandiloquent conception, the audience makes no demands on Lady Gregory's style. Her simple diction, her lucid sentence structure, and her easy flowing rhythms are both appropriate and effective. O'Duffy's play, by its very largeness of conception, demands an appropriate grandeur of expression, and this it most distinctly lacks. Like Maxwell Anderson's historical dramas, it demands more style than its author could give it. It is written in a straightforward, unbrogued prose, peppered with neo-Shakespearean archaisms. Although clear, fluent enough, and perhaps, if it were in a different kind of play, even adequate, the writing has neither power nor lyricism nor evocative appeal. One might as well try to write *Areopagitica* in, say, the ordinary expository style of O'Flaherty or O'Faolain.

The chief qualities of the play are two—a well-defined theme arises from the welter of events, and the characterization of the thoughtful Malachy is excellent. Malachy, although his basic dramatic purpose is completed by the end of Act III, is a sane intelligence in a world of greed, passion, and stupidity. It is an adroit bit of work to have made him so impressive when he is surrounded by more obviously theatrical characters, all being swept by storms of passion, cupidity, and violence.

Malachy the Great has one serious difficulty in structure—the fact that the main character has little of significance to do in the last two acts—but its virtues are abundant, and its great fault of style might well have been minimized by the theatrical values of a vivid production. Many worse plays have been staged, and 1933 was not exactly a bumper year for genius in the Irish theatre. There would be no huge point in resurrecting this play for current production, however. Although it is definitely interesting, it is hardly a lost work of genius. (Nevertheless, it is interesting to note that Tom Kilroy's *The O'Neill,* an historical play whose faults and virtues are precisely those of *Malachy the Great,* was performed recently with very considerable success by the Abbey in the Peacock Theatre).

II

The Wasted Island is O'Duffy's first major work. As it was originally published in 1919, and as its culminating incident was the Easter Rising, it is safe to assume that the bulk of it was written when O'Duffy was in his early and middle twenties—that is, in the two or three years immediately following the Rising. The 1919 version was issued by the short-lived Dublin publishing firm of Martin Lester, Ltd. Its directors were Bulmer Hobson, James MacNeill, and Colm O'Lochlainn, whose later notable Three Candles Press is still active.

Vivian Mercier condemns the novel out of hand:

> The interest of *The Wasted Island* is historical only; it shows how a member of the Volunteers could hate and mistrust the Pearse clique, the more so for having known some of them intimately, and could still in 1919 regard the 1916 Rising as a criminal error. Even in the revised version of 1929 the style is full of cliches, while characterisation just does not exist, except in the case of the central figure, who is O'Duffy himself.

P. S. O'Hegarty feels, on the other hand, that the book

> . . . is one of the best of modern Irish novels. It is a young man's book, full of the tumultuousness of the times, full of things he had experienced and felt, full

of actuality. It contains too faithful a portrayal of some of the 1916 leaders, and too faithful a portrayal of the seething pot out of which the Rising came, to be popular, but it will come into its own in time.

There is really little to compare this book to in modern Irish literature. Michael Farrell's *Thy Tears Might Cease* comes to mind, but *The Wasted Island* is something more than the conventional *bildungsroman.* Of course, it is a coming-of-age novel in which the hero's life is traced from his birth, through his schooldays, through his university career, and to his final insanity which is brought about largely by the character of his society and the events of his time. However, this is a coming-of-age novel which is couched in basically political terms. We get, naturally, the inevitable incidents of the *bildungsroman,* such as the hero's relations with his parents, his attitude toward his education, his love affairs, and his general thoughts about life. But his spiritual and mental growth is mainly measured by his political education, rather than—as is more usual—by his opinions about love or God or the nature of the good life.

Bernard Lascelles is the oldest son of a prominent Establishment physician, but although his father has all of the predictable Anglo-Irish opinions, his mother is Roman Catholic, and so the boy from the beginning has a somewhat divided view. He is sent to an English boarding school, Ashbury, which is both Catholic and upper class, and so, although he is an Irish Catholic, he has been like the typical West Briton well insulated against any significant knowledge of Ireland and its history. Bernard's school, although Catholic, is still a version of the English public school, and O'Duffy's critical dissection of its faults is a worthy antidote to the uncritical enthusiasms of Thomas Hughes and Rudyard Kipling. Ashbury's indoctrination of the Establishment virtues quite fails with Bernard, and the school's real effect is to push him into Socialist views.

Upon graduation, Bernard's natural course would have been to enter Oxford, but his father's moderate income and high standard of living force him to return to Dublin. There, largely through a desire to be perverse and to irritate his father, he declines to enter Trinity, and goes instead to the National University. It is there that his education enters a new phase.

Nominally studying medicine, Bernard's real education comes from his fellow students who represent various attitudes towards Irish nationalism. The novel is in no sense jingoistic, however, and Bernard's education in the history of his country is no stupid or total or immediate conversion. Indeed, this lengthy section of the book is a balanced, thorough, and absorbing depiction of the Irish intellectual milieu at one of the most crucial times in its history. But despite its power as narrative and its engrossing depiction of manners, the viewpoint of the book was hardly calculated to make it a success with either the English public or the prevailing sentiment of the Irish public after the executions that followed the Easter Rising. My copy of the English edition, for instance, has many outraged Colonel Blimpish marginal comments, which some previous owner made about the author's pro-Irish sentiments. Moreover, the view that the Rising was a tragic error made by misguided and hysterical idealists was not one that most Irishmen would have sympathized with in 1919. It was certainly the view of most of the country during the Rising, but the week of executions transformed all utterly, and a terrible beauty was born.

O'Duffy, like his hero, was active in the Irish Volunteers and supported Eoin MacNeill's moderate policy. This view may be seen in the treatment of Padraic Pearse who appears under the name of Austin Mallow, a somewhat mystic poet with an almost masochistic desire for martyrdom. The hysteria of Mallow's exhortations to the Irish to fight has much of the flavor of, say, Pearse's oration at the grave of O'Donovan Rossa, portions of which were used in a similarly critical fashion by O'Casey in *The Plough and the Stars.* The yearning for martyrdom which appears in Mallow is certainly apparent in various works by Pearse—his play *The Singer,* for instance.

Nevertheless, Yeats was right in "Easter 1916," and, indeed, in one short passage late in the novel O'Duffy admits the fact that the heroic deaths of the leaders of the Rising had ennobled a ghastly fiasco. He does not quite admit, even in his revision of the novel ten years later, the fact that the executions had solidified Irish opinion into resistance and had transformed a fiasco into a triumph. Indeed, his novel, even in its revised version, still ends with a remark by the secondary hero that now they must begin all over again from nothing.

So although *The Wasted Island* was to a large segment of the Irish nation as unpalatable a statement as was *The Plough and the Stars* a few years later, there yet remains the considerable achievement of having depicted accurately the sentiments of a significant segment of the Irish leadership. Indeed, the novel is a vivid evocation of all significant cross-sections of Irish political thought in the first twelve or fifteen years of the century. O'Duffy's principal method of dramatizing this complex and shifting series of opinions is by a series of heated dialogues which are dotted throughout the novel. It is difficult to extrapolate any short segment from these extended arguments, but the following short excerpt on *The Playboy* row will give something of their general flavor. The Mallow in the passage is probably based on Willie Pearse.

"You're not far out," replied Mallow. "I've been down at the Abbey, hooting the *Playboy*."

"Good Lord!" ejaculated Manders. "I thought that sort of thing was out of date now."

"Nothing is ever out of date in this remarkable island," said Crowley. "To what end was the cachinnation, dearie?"

"The play's an insult to the country," said Mallow. "It makes us all out to be a lot of parricides."

"How dreadful!" said Crowley.

"And there was a fellow talking about girls in their shifts," went on Mallow, not heeding the sarcasm.

"So long as it wasn't their pants–," interjected McGurk.

"Tut-tut, Hugo," said Crowley. "A true Irishman doesn't know about such things."

"Well, I call it disgusting," said Mallow.

"What? To wear a shift?"

"Get away with you," said Mallow sourly. "What call had they to bring it into a play?"

"So you registered your protest in the popular fashion?"

"I stood up–," said Mallow.

"High upon the gallows tree–."

"Ah, shut up. I stood up and I said: 'This play's a disgrace to the country', so I did. But the rotten cowards had a peeler waiting outside, and he came and threw me out."

"Tilly," said Crowley to the waitress, who had come up with his order, "this gentleman has just been martyred for Faith and Fatherland. Bring him some tea at my expense."

Or probably a more typical excerpt would be the following which is directly about politics:

> "The party," he said, "have a big responsibility. They can't leave the control of a movement like the Volunteers in the hands of a few extremists."
>
> O'Dwyer gave a snort of contempt. "That word 'extremist.' What the devil do you think it means? It's just the muddle-headed sort of cliché the English like. What you really mean when you say 'extremists' is 'separatists.' "
>
> "Well, they are extremists, aren't they?"
>
> "Of course, but not more than other people. Redmond's an extremist. Horace Plunkett's an extremist—."
>
> "Oh, get away!"
>
> "Yes. An extreme Home Ruler and an extreme Cooperator. They wouldn't be much use if they were only moderate ones, would they?"
>
> "You're only playing with words," said Eugene.
>
> "No, I'm not. It's you that are misusing them. When you call us extremists you think of us as desperate fellows who like fighting for its own sake. Well, we aren't. I'm all for peace. I want to get this question settled once for all, not left at loose ends, so that I can chuck politics and get at my writing. I can't fiddle while my country falls, but I wish she'd stop falling so that I might have a chance to do some fiddling."

What O'Duffy finally succeeds in doing by many passages like these is to document faithfully and also to give a strong sense of immediacy to the intellectual currents of his time. The novel, among other things, is a painless and vividly dramatized course in Irish history.

The final view of the novel is reminiscent of the final view of *The Plough and the Stars.* A terrible sense of desolation and of waste has grown throughout the book. It has grown, even through the satire, the humor, the comedy of manners, the heroics of the Howth gun running, and the charms and agonies of the love story;

and it culminates in the tragic power of the conclusion, the Rising and its aftermath.

Bernard and his friends stay apart from the Rising, but finally he is driven out to help, kills a soldier, flees in revulsion, is apprehended by the English and thrown into a cell. There, because of the intolerable conditions of his public life and his personal life (when he was earlier in prison, his fiancée had jilted him for an English soldier), he goes mad.

Although I hardly agree with Benedict Kiely that *The Wasted Island* is dull, it is far from a perfect book. At times it even approaches the faults of a bad popular novel. Mercier thinks that the style of the original version would do no credit to the "Ballyslapguttery Notes" in a provincial paper, and that the style of the revision was not inordinately improved. Undoubtedly the style of the original version does have its lame moments, and throughout it is too quick and careless. I do not myself think that the style of the original version was bad enough to be a major flaw, or even in many passages to be a distraction. When O'Duffy revised the book in 1929, he was fairly thorough, except for the last fifty pages which remain virtually unchanged. His revision consists mainly in a more logical arrangement of some incidents, and in considerable deletion and addition of detail and auctorial comment. Usually, he seems to have eliminated detail which was flat, gauche, or insignificant, and to have added detail which is terser or more evocative. His editing of auctorial comments tends to omit the stilted, and also to add a more specific treatment of the historical background. The stylistic improvements are fairly numerous and consist largely in the pruning of unnecessary words and in the occasional substitution of more appropriate ones. The only real change in the novel's original view is a softening of the earlier caustic tone toward the hero's father. In general, it may be said that O'Duffy improved the book in a multitude of minor ways, but that he made no major changes.

Mercier is probably right in his charge that the characters are thinly drawn, but it should be remembered that the novel is painted on a very large canvas with a cast of characters that is almost huge. O'Duffy handles characterization, then, rather like the playwright, by drawing in an accurate silhouette rather than by painting over every inch of the space. His intention was not to write a series of profound psychological studies, although the character of his hero is excellently realized; his intention was to limn a portrait of the manners of a whole society and to re-create the whole spectrum of political ideas of the time. His portrait of manners is carried off with a mature, witty, and discerning eye; and his political discussions are exact, thorough, and absorbing. With such excellently achieved qualities, the faults of the book diminish rather perceptibly.

A usual cliché about Irish fiction is that it has produced a remarkable galaxy of brilliant short story writers, but very few novelists. Like any cliché, this one has some basis in fact, but it is hardly the whole truth. Frank O'Connor wrote somewhere that after O'Casey writers like O'Flaherty, O'Faolain, Mary Lavin, and himself "turned from the theatre and adopted fiction—mainly the short story—as our medium." The fact that four of the best writers who succeeded O'Casey were much more at ease in short fiction than in the novel has probably obscured the fact that there have always been important and weighty novelists in Ireland. In *The Wasted Island,* one of the characters laments the spate of little plays and little stories and little poems thrown up by the Irish Renaissance, and points out that previously Irish literature has been full of big things—from the *Tain* to the *Annals of the Four Masters* to *The Midnight Court* and to Carleton and Kickham. This certainly was also O'Duffy's view, and in this novel he has attempted to do a big thing.

To my mind, he has done it. He has done it imperfectly; he has been in it too much of the snarling Bricriu for his own success; but, nevertheless, after the passage of fifty years, this remains an absorbing and moving novel, which I think is important enough to be ranked with *The Lake, The Crock of Gold, The Charwoman's Daughter, The Portrait of the Artist,* and *Ulysses* in any history of Irish fiction. A tradition which throws up six such brilliant and disparate works in a twenty-year period can hardly be said to be impoverished.

Printer's Errors, O'Duffy's second novel, appeared before book publication as a serial in *The Freeman's Journal,* and was then issued separately by Martin Lester. O'Duffy, in a letter of February 9, 1922, contained in the National Library of Ireland, remarked to Bulmer Hobson, "I'm ready to bet any money that all the reviewers will comment on the singular appropriateness of the title, for the book positively abounds in misprints."

O'Duffy calls the novel "a little jeu d'esprit." But Mercier remarks of it, "Any keen student of the aberrations of genius should take a quick look at a 'novel' by

O'Duffy called *Printer's Errors*." O'Hegarty remarks, "His second novel *Printer's Errors* (1922) is one for which I have a great affection, though the purists sniff at it. It is a light satirical comedy of love and laughter, with excellent character drawings, and deserves a wider circulation."

A *jeu d'esprit*, I take it, is a work of no particular thematic significance, but of some claim to charm, playfulness, and inventiveness. It exists not merely to entertain, but to entertain delightfully. However, one man's *jeu* is often another man's *peu*, and it is quite impossible to prove to somebody that he should be charmed when he is not. T. E. Eliot regarded Hawthorne's *The House of the Seven Gables* as a book of great charm, but it has always seemed to me one of the five or six most dismal books ever written. Such favorite *jeux d'esprit* of mine as J. R. R. Tolkien's *The Hobbit* or Mervyn Wall's *The Unfortunate Fursey* have been found by certain people whose taste I respect to be too unbearable to finish. Consequently, I cannot hope to persuade anybody that *Printer's Errors* is delightful, but only to give my own requirements for delight. *The Hobbit* and *The Unfortunate Fursey* I would use as touchstones, and O'Duffy's book does not have their high quality of inventiveness. He does not create, as they do, a unique world of his own. However, there is certainly one other type of *jeu d'esprit* which, if it does not attempt the high inventiveness of creating its own world, does succeed in pervading an ordinary milieu with delight. There is the pervasive geniality and humor in such books as, say, *The Wrong Box* by Robert Louis Stevenson and Lloyd Osborne, or *Antigua Penny Puce* by Robert Graves, or the early stories and plays of William Saroyan, that make these works inimitable, and rereadable with little diminution of their original effect. That inimitable quality comes, I think, not from the creation of some unique never-never land, but from the ordinary world being pervaded by the author's inimitable personality.

It is to this second group that *Printer's Errors* belongs. It is not, to my mind, quite on a par with Graves's delicious novel, but it probably succeeds as much as the Stevenson and Osborne. It is the story of a middle-aged printer of no particular brilliance, who throws over the conventions in search of love and adventure. And if he does not finally get the beautiful girl he had his heart set on, he does succeed in getting one much more comfortable and suited to him. He also succeeds in getting abducted not by pirates (which would, of course, have been ideal), but by swindlers (which is nearly as good). If he does not manage to get marooned on a desert island, he is at least deserted on Ireland's Eye, off Howth harbor.

Along the way, O'Duffy includes some droll satirical shafts at the Dublin intelligentsia and the Dublin theatre. The book has here a mildly Philistine tone which I find less admirable than the author probably intended. However our attention is claimed chiefly by the engaging spectacle of conventional people discovering their own warm humanity which has previously been inhibited by stuffy social codes. The printer's son is a fine, broad comic character, who fancies himself the Superman, but who is eventually caught, like Shaw's John Tanner, by an irresistible woman. Among the minor characters is a poet named Lucius Loftus, who seems to be a cartoon of O'Duffy himself. Loftus is regarded with suspicion by the galaxy of poets and critics who contribute to *The Exotic Review,* or who attend the productions of The Eclectic Theatre, because his work is enjoyed by ordinary people. Loftus himself occasionally goes out of his way to guy the literary establishment. Once, before a sombre meeting of a branch of the Gaelic League, he passes off a ridiculous parody of his own as an authentic Irish song. On another occasion he secures a production of a play of his at the Eclectic Theatre by subtitling it a psycho-allegorical comedy. "The play," he explains to the printer, "is a mere lighthearted comedy, but if I hadn't called it psycho-something it would never have been accepted by this temple of the muses." This portion of the novel is a deft, light satire about the preoccupations of Edward Martyn's Irish Theatre, which was interested in Ibsen, Chekhov, and Strindberg, but which did produce two of O'Duffy's own plays.

The comedy of the book is so nicely of a piece that it is difficult to pick a section to exemplify it. My favorite is a droll pirate playlet staged as part of a charade, but, as it is a bit long, the following collision of the printer with the direct method of teaching Irish will serve to give the flavor of the comedy.

> Soon afterwards F. F. joined the League and began to learn Irish. . . . His class consisted of two bright schoolboys, a middle-aged lady, an old man, a young man and a young girl (evidently lovers) and himself. They were taught by a young man named Conchubhar Ó Galchabhair, who had long hair and wild-looking eyes, and who used the Módh Díreach enthusiastically and unintelligently.
>
> "Bhosca," he would say, placing a large box on the table in front of him.
>
> "Bhosca," they would all repeat.

Then he would say in a tone of eager interrogation: "An bhosca é?"

So far so good. But there were snags ahead.

"Sé sin mo bhosca," he said. Then to Mr. Wolverhampton, "A Fréderic, an é sin mo bhosca?"

"Seadh. Sé sin mo bhosca."

"O, ní h'eadh! Ní h'eadh! Ní hé sin do bhosca. Sé sin mo bhosca."

"That's what I *said,*" cried F. F. "I *said* mo bhosca."

"Anois, anois! Ná h-abair é as Beurla, má is é do thoil é. Ní hé sin do bhosca; sé sin mo bhosca."

"Exactly," said F. F. "Sé sin mo bhosca."

Conchubhar was exasperated. He handed the box to F. F. and said: *"Do* bhosca." Then he took it back and said, *"mo* bhosca."

Then he handed it again to F. F. and said:

"Sé sin do bhosca. Anois, an é sin do bhosca."

"Seadh," said F. F. shirking the difficulty.

"Seadh sé sin . . ." with an interrogative tone.

"Do bhosca," said F. F.

"Tut-tut," said Conchubhar, which is no language at all, so it was still Módh Direach. He thought for a moment, seemed to swear under his breath, and, flinging Módh Direach to the winds, said:

"Can't you understand? 'Mo is my' and 'do is your.' "

"Oh, I see," said F. F., "and what does all the rest of it mean?"

This gentle satire, Horatian rather than Juvenalian, is what pervades the book. The comedy of the novel into which this satire is threaded is the version of romance that one might expect from an optimistic realist. The book is not ambitious and not quite so irresistible as a really superb *jeu d'esprit* should be, but it at least is so pleasantly attractive that one wishes it were longer.

O'Duffy wrote his next novel, *The Lion and the Fox,* in the winter of 1921–1922, when he was apparently teaching at Mount St. Benedict in Gorey. He was now married, and the first of his two children had been born. The winter was a hard one, he had little money, and his remarks to Bulmer Hobson show him frantically writing letters to find himself a job back in Dublin. For one of his political background, the prospects were hardly promising. As he wrote on March 6, 1922:

> There are few jobs and most of them are gratis, & anyway she [the wife of Desmond Fitzgerald] fears *The Wasted Island* won't help me to anything. . . . I'm surprised to hear business is so bad, but I suppose it is inevitable until de Valera & his pack of donkeys are put in their place. We're quite out of touch with politics here, but I'm sure the country regards them as I do, as a lot of damned nuisances.

In May, he did finally manage to get a job in Dublin, and at the end of the month he moved his family into "a very nice, tho' expensive flat at 14 Up. Fitzwilliam Street."

One of his earliest comments about *The Lion and the Fox* was in a letter to Hobson of July 4, 1921. He wrote:

> I don't think the O'Neill story will exceed 80,000, but it will certainly attain it. Don't be alarmed about its quality. I started out with the idea of making it a potboiler, but I got so enraptured with my materials (the State papers, etc.) that I have changed all that. I am putting my best into the book, and yet I think it should be popular. It should run well as a serial, for it is crowded with incident: fights, flights, intrigues, and what not, and each chapter (they average 3000 words) ends with a snap.

Had O'Duffy used a pseudonym on the title page of *The Lion and the Fox,* no one would ever have attributed the book to him. It is, as he says, a swashbuckling historical novel, full of battles, romance and intrigue, and quite unlike anything else he ever wrote. There is in it no hint of the satirist and but little of the humorist. It is something of an Irish equivalent of *The Three Musketeers,* hardly as memorable as Dumas's masterpiece, but not withered by the comparison.

The story tells of a part of Elizabeth's Irish wars and is set at the end of the sixteenth and the beginning of the seventeenth century. Although at first the story seems as casually episodic as Dumas, the individual episodes finally all fall into place to tell of the rise and fall of the short-lived Munster Confederacy. The first hundred or so pages are a kind of quest. During a truce, four young men are sent by the Ulster leader Hugh O'Neill to unify the bickering and divided Munster chiefs. The envoys have some measure of success and manage to effect an uneasy coalition of the leaders and to put a formidable force into the field. For a time the confederacy is effective and succeeds in expelling the English from most of Munster. However, the enterprise was from the first doomed to dissolve into factional jealousies, for the Ulster envoys did not succeed in winning the unqualified support of the one man able to unify the province, Florence MacCarthy. Without MacCarthy, the movement breaks up into intrigues and treacheries, the leaders are dispersed or captured, "but the Ulstermen, with hopeful and resolute hearts, turned their backs upon the province and marched away to the battlefields of the North."

Within this broad outline of plot, there are four or five more or less self-contained episodes developed at length, but somewhat different in tone. Cormac's first attempt to see MacCarthy is an intrigue plot, initially frustrated by the Milady DeWinter-like figure of MacCarthy's wife, the Lady Ellen, and involving the Richelieu-like figure of Miler MacGrath, the Protestant Archbishop of Cashel. There are a couple of episodes which culminate heroically in beautifully handled battle scenes. There is Art O'Cahan's interlude of spying in Cork, and there is the romantic skullduggery of rescuing Owen's fiancée from the English stronghold, and finally there is the frantic last attempt to win MacCarthy's allegiance and the dismal breakup of the confederacy.

One fault of the novel is its characterization, although "fault" may be too strong a word, for the characterization is less bad than scanty. Undoubtedly the reason is that the book, like *The Wasted Island,* has a very large cast of historical characters, and most of them are necessarily sketched in by the dramatist's method of the hasty silhouette. Given the medium length of the novel, this method was unavoidable, and so perhaps it would be more proper to say that O'Duffy wrote too short a book for his material.

O'Duffy's Irish musketeers are Art O'Cahan, Cormac O'Neill, Owen O'Ruairc, and Conn MacSweeny. Art, in his late thirties, is the oldest and canniest of the group and its Athos. Cormac, who grows from hotheaded rashness to wise maturity, is the D'Artagnan figure, and the character with whom the reader most identifies. Owen, the dapper lover, is the Aramis, and the phlegmatic MacSweeny is the Porthos, but these two characters are, like Aramis and Porthos, given less and less space as the novel progresses. Indeed, even Art's death is related briefly at second-hand, as Cormac becomes increasingly the chief character. But even though Cormac is the chief figure in the book, he is not really its protagonist, and this, I think, is the novel's second major flaw.

The protagonist is the complex, contradictory and fascinating Florence MacCarthy, and the story is as much a book-long combat for his support as it is the account of the rise and decline of a rebellion. MacCarthy is pushed into prominence not only because of the constantly expressed and conflicting attitudes of the other characters toward him, but also because the story's crucial decision is his to make. He is regarded with suspicion and fondness often by the same individuals. He seems both subtle and blunt, amiable and sinister, patriotic and self-seeking, brave and cowardly; in effect, he seems an enigma. This enigmatical quality is certainly part of O'Duffy's strategy, for it maintains the tension of the story by prolonging MacCarthy's decision until the very end. Yet MacCarthy can only remain an enigma as long as he is kept offstage for long periods, and indeed he is allowed only a handful of major scenes in the book's nearly three hundred pages.

My feeling is that O'Duffy made a strategic error here. The uncertainty and tension which he sought is only spurious, for it would take a very uninformed reader to imagine that the Irish won this contest. Also, just in terms of the novel, great effect is lost by keeping the protagonist in the background. MacCarthy could easily have been a tragic figure in the foreground, whose agony of indecision is explored and probed. But instead of tragedy, O'Duffy elected to give us romance, adventure and intrigue involving what should have been only minor characters in the plot. Although Dumas also in *The Three Musketeers* elected to relate his story of the Queen, Buckingham and Richelieu by the adventures of such essentially peripheral figures as D'Artagnan, the Musketeers and Milady, his story was not in the least harmed, for its core was only an intrigue. In O'Duffy's novel, the core of the story is a tragedy, and it is only when the novel is finished that the reader realizes its incidents were but diversionary tactics; and that the real center of the book was not written.

The book's narrative prose has only minor stiffnesses, which are so unnoticed in the flow and surge of events as to be trivial. Basically, the prose is effective, spare and muscular. A high proportion of the story is told in dialogue which is pervaded with enough unobtrusive archaisms to give the flavor of the time without impeding the swiftness of the narration. At points, as in the following curse scene upon a traitor, the prose even rises to considerable dramatic eloquence:

> The party went rapidly down the slope, the unfortunate Earl stumbling ever and again in his shackles. The Bishop dauntlessly scrabbled after them, intent on making a last appeal; but the pace was too fast, the way too rugged for his famished and aged limbs. He stopped at last, almost exhausted; then, summoning the last of his strength, he stood upon a ledge of rock, erect, rigid, his hands raised to heaven, and his white hair streaming in the wind.
>
> "On, Edmund FitzGibbon," he cried. "Carry your brother to the slaughterhouse of the butchers that have bought him. Fetch home your blood-money and gloat upon it in the night. Grasp all the happiness that your mean soul covets, for your time is short. The curse of God is upon you, Edmund FitzGibbon. Living you shall be loathed among living men, and dying you shall perish in infamy. The name of your house shall cease,

and your race shall vanish from the earth. The springs of repentance and hope shall be dried up in your soul, and your heart shall wither in your last hour. The thief shall find pardon, and the adulterer shall find pardon; yea, the guilt of the murderer shall be washed away. But you shall freeze eternally in hell's centre; for there is no anger but abates except the anger of Christ with Clan Gibbon."

The Bishop's head sank exhausted on his breast and his arms dropped to his sides. A sardonic laugh echoed back among the crags.

This is a difficult volume to sum up. It is an impressive artistic achievement to have marshalled such a large cast and such a complicated series of remote events into a satisfying narrative. The book is better and more important than any of O'Duffy's save *The Wasted Island* and the first two volumes of the Cuanduine trilogy, and if I have praised it with faint damns the reason is that it contained the seeds of something more imposing than the merely first-rate adventure yarn.

In *Miss Rudd and Some Lovers,* O'Duffy does not try for any major statement of theme or for any sweeping historical scope. Like *Printer's Errors,* the book is basically an entertainment, a charming and successful minor novel which was meant for a pleasant bedside book. Although it is set in Dublin during the Black and Tan war, although there are raids and skirmishes in the streets, and although the heroine is even sentenced by the military authorities to six months in prison, the volume is by no means another *Wasted Island.* The political events serve simply as the sombre background for a lighthearted story.

The story is told in the first person by Miss Anastasia Rudd, a bright and self-possessed young woman who turns to writing popular romantic fiction under the pseudonym of Lucy Loveday, in order to extricate herself from the low-paying drudgery of office work. The plot, such as it is, concerns her attempt to gain some experience of life so that her next novel will have, as her publisher phrases it, "the necessary touch of passion." By a series of awkward misunderstandings, she finds herself engaged to a handsome, but vulgar and stupid, young man who is interested mainly in her money, and much of the mildly absurd plot depicts her efforts to extricate herself from the engagement.

The plot is sufficient to keep the book ambling along, but the real excellence of the volume is its characterization and its satire. O'Duffy provides a series of deftly, whimsically observed views of lower-middle-class Dublin in 1922. His scenes around the boarding house dinner table are carried off with an almost Dickensian flair. They are lovingly and fully developed, and three or four of the characters are fine, solid, full-bodied comic creations. Mrs. Buck, the landlady whose conversation is constantly punctuated with memories of her late husband, is a worthy sister of Mrs. Micawber. For instance:

> "I always think there's nothing half as nice as a nicely poached egg," said Mrs. Buck. "Poor Buck (R. I. P.) thought the same. Always had one to his breakfast every morning of his life. Never asked for a bit of bacon because his stomach was bad, but *would not* do without his egg, even to his last day. I remember that morning still. 'Not a second more than three minutes,' says he, weak like. And when I came up there he was gone to heaven, and he without his breakfast. I always regretted not being in time to give it to him. Don't ye know, I

think it's uncomfortable like, dying on an empty stomach. . . ."

Then there is the young wit, with the consummately Dickensian name of Freddie Slapjuice, who is courting Mrs. Buck's daughter, and who is addicted to humorous sallies like "I beg your puddings." And there is the superb Mr. Kinsella, a mournful drunkard who combines the most annoying qualities of Handy Andy and The Ancient Mariner. There is Miss Rudd's brother Bill, an ex M.P., who was directed into politics because he was the booby of the family, and who is so inordinately anxious to please that he follows one fulsome compliment with three or four more even more extravagant. When introduced as a marriageable prospect by Mrs. Buck to her daughter Violet, he remarks:

> "A beautiful girl, Mrs. Buck," said Bill. "Charming! Wonderful! Magnificent! Finest girl I ever saw in my life. . . ." In the pause I knew he was seeking for some feature to praise: Bill was incapable of letting well alone. Then, "What a splendid big mouth she's got!" he declared with enthusiasm.

Like *Printer's Errors,* this is an unassuming and genial tale. In it O'Duffy's humor and sense of fun, which came to be overwhelmed by the serious satiric purpose of his later work, gets full play. Some of his constant qualities, however, can be seen in the book. His sense of economic injustice appears implicitly but strongly in several places. For instance, one of Miss Rudd's friends is Oliver Carney, a playwright and novelist of real ability, who is only able to eke out the most marginal existence for his burgeoning family and who lives in a kind of hand to mouth squalor. While Carney's real talent is practically unmarketable, Miss Rudd's worthless potboilers manage to give her a handsome independence. It is difficult not to see a glumly personal note here.

As O'Duffy was initially a humorist, there was of necessity considerable of the realist in his makeup. Even the romantic comedy of *Printer's Errors* has the realistic foundation of the humorist. In *Miss Rudd,* there is again the realist's view of romance. Miss Rudd is not a giddy young woman, but a sensible and level-headed one, interested in men but not dazzled by most of those around her. The romantic novels that she writes she regards as sentimental tosh for silly young girls and sloppy youths of seventeen. The one eligible male in the book who is good enough for her does come moderately close to sweeping her off her feet, but when O'Duffy has him become interested in someone else Miss Rudd sensibly takes the matter with a mature calm. There would certainly be, in this genial and easy tale, a final pleasure in having the heroine married off. Miss Rudd is an Elizabeth Bennett kind of character, not so beautiful or vivacious as some of the other young women in the book, but she has, nevertheless, all of the intelligent reader's sympathy. And perhaps because O'Duffy is really writing a droll tale for the intelligent reader, he feels that he can dispense with the conventional romantic ending of an attractive marriage for the heroine.

Although she is a convincingly drawn young woman, I think that there is a good deal of O'Duffy in Miss Rudd, but there is probably another facet of his character embodied in her brother Rudolph, many of whose characteristics are quite reminiscent also of Edward Connolly, the imperturbable engineer of Bernard Shaw's novel *The Irrational Knot.* Rudolph is a brilliant inventor, with a Shavian insouciance about marriage, but his caustic summation of actuality is somewhat tempered by a delightfully adolescent streak of romanticism. It is his harebrained scheme to rescue Miss Rudd's fiancé, Horace Tackaberry, from military prison that causes his sister and himself to be apprehended. He, incidentally, had been the cause of Tackaberry's imprisonment, for he lodged false information about Tackaberry with the military, in order to rid his sister of unwelcome attentions.

There are one or two minor touches in this novel that are just a bit eccentric. O'Duffy's father was a well-known Dublin dentist, and O'Duffy himself had been trained as a dentist. There are a number of ill-tempered references to ill-fitting and ugly false teeth in the novel, which have been fashioned by quack dentists. And one of Miss Rudd's lovers mysteriously disappears early in the story because he, as we later discover, has grown ashamed of being a quack dentist, and has determined to get a bona-fide degree so that he may be worthy of Miss Rudd. These bits have actually so little to do with anything else in the book that they seem just faintly mad.

This vein of humorous and genial satire, which O'Duffy mined in *Printer's Errors* and in *Miss Rudd and Some Lovers,* was one which he did consummately. He developed beyond it, however, into the serious satire of his trilogy. In that development, even though the first two volumes of the trilogy are masterly, much of this gentle good humor was lost. The books that succeeded these early comedies are entirely on a higher plane of value, but one must still regret that the emergence of a brilliant satirist so thoroughly displaced the charming humorist.

III

King Goshawk and the Birds is the first volume of O'Duffy's great trilogy. With the Fursey books of Mervyn Wall and the Adam books of Conal O'Riordan, it strongly disproves the cliché that, save for the magnificent exception of James Joyce, Ireland lacks sustained and memorable work in the novel form.

King Goshawk is a satiric fantasy, set at some time in the future when the world, worsened much beyond its present state, has been devastated and subjected to the rule of a few King Capitalists who control its wealth. One of these King Capitalists, Goshawk, decides to buy up all of the birds and flowers for his wife, Guzzelinda. To combat this, an old Dublin philosopher brings Cuchulain back to earth, and Cuchulain, after a series of droll misadventures, agrees to sire a son who will right things. The son is Cuanduine, and his adventures take up two-thirds of the book. The satire is quite broad, a kind of caricature really, but the prose style is so easy and fluent and the invention is so unflaggingly fertile, that the book is compulsively readable.

The genial, easy humor of O'Duffy's two light novels is still apparent in the early section of the book, which relates the collisions of the heroic Cuchulain with the very unheroic modern world. For instance:

> You should have seen Cuchulain playing tennis with the gentry and ladies of the Bon Ton suburb. He learnt the whole art and skill of the game in ten minutes, and straightway beat the Champion of all Ireland six-love, six-love, and six-love. Never had such strength and agility been seen before. He could cross the court in one leap; he never served a fault, and none but the Champion ever returned his service; he would take any stroke on the volley; and at the net his smash invariably burst the ball.

The book has so many fine things like this that it is difficult to describe, but above all it is a *reductio ad absurdum* of capitalist premises. The brave new world which it posits is one in which capitalism has run rampant, and created a ghastly, vulgar, tawdry wasteland for the many, and a millionaire's ghetto of delights for the few. The details of this world are worked out with unflagging ingenuity; and although the book definitely proselytizes for a certain view of economics, the message is divertingly dramatized and never for an instant slips into the hectoring overtones that mar the final volume of the trilogy.

The view of the modern world in *King Goshawk* has some affinities with the views of Brecht and Kafka, but the humorist is usually in command of the satirist, and the most caustic points are still made with a paradoxically light touch. Even when O'Duffy's satire becomes particularly mordant, he is practically always saved by his form from shrillness and hysteria. Here, for example, are two paragraphs which describe Cuchulain's first view of modern Dublin:

> What ruin and decay were here: what filth and litter: what nauseating stenches. The houses were so crazy with age and so shaken with bombardments that there was scarce one that could stand without assistance: therefore they were held together by plates and rivets, or held apart by cross-beams, or braced up by scaffoldings, so that the street had the appearance of a dead forest. (Was it not a strange perversity that slew the living tree to lengthen the days of these tottering skeletons?) Many of the houses were roofless; others were inhabited only in their lower storeys; some had collapsed altogether, and squatters had built them huts of wood or mud or patchwork on the hard-pounded rubble. The streets were ankle-deep in dung and mire; craters yawned in their midst; piles of wrecked masonry obstructed them. Rivulets ran where the gutters had been. Foul sewer smells issued from holes and cracks.
>
> Fit lairage was this for the tragomaschaloid mob that jostled the celestial visitor to the realms of earth. What stink of breath and body assailed his nostrils; what debased accents, raucous voices, and evil language offended his hearing; what grime, what running sores, what raw-rimmed eye-sockets, what gum-suppuration and tooth-rot, what cavernous cheeks, what leering lips and hopeless eyes, what pain-twisted faces, what sagging spines, what streeling steps, what filthy ragged raiment covering what ghastly-imagined hideousness of body sickened his beauty-nurtured sight.

What, of course, saves—indeed, what enhances—this passage and makes it memorable is not the content, but the imaginative detail, the evocative diction, and the firmly controlled sentence structure.

O'Duffy was from the beginning a fluent prose writer, but the prose of *The Wasted Island* had its stilted and turgid moments which only the intensity of the content or the sweep of the narrative made bearable. Here, however, O'Duffy's prose has taken a great salmon leap, and there is passage after passage in this book that bears comparison to the style of O'Duffy's masters, who were

Martial, Rabelais, Voltaire, Jonathan Swift, Samuel Butler, and Bernard Shaw.

What in this volume O'Duffy shares in common with these great satirists is not only a rage of disgust with man's folly, but also a joyous relish in form. Although he spreads his shots widely, attacking not only from the base of an economic theory, but also from the broader base of the moralist's disgust with perennial human folly, he never loses control. His rage never becomes unbridled, and his rhetoric never slips into slovenliness or hysterical rant. In fact, despite the ferocious intensity of much of his attack, his joyous creative inventiveness gives him a superb balance. He is able, as even Swift was always not in the great last book of *Gulliver's Travels,* to write something not for its content but for its form. He was able to compose a passage not because what it says is an irreproachable condemnation (or is, in fact, even at the moment relevant), but because it in itself is excellent. As a case in point, consider the following delicious paragraph which attacks nothing at all:

> Now when the Manager of MacWhatsisname's grocery saw Cuchulain facing him in the same dreadful guise wherein he overcame Ferdiad at the ford and drove Fergus before him from the field of Gairech, the strength went out of his limbs, and the corpuscles of his blood fled in disgraceful rout to seek refuge in the inmost marrow of his bones. Dreadful were the scenes that were then enacted in the arched and slippery dark purple passages of his venous system. Smitten with a common panic, Red Cells, Lymphocytes, and Phagocytes rushed in headlong confusion down the peripheral veins, which soon became choked with swarming struggling masses of fugitives. Millions of smaller Lymphocytes and Mast Cells perished in the crush, but the immense mobs poured on towards the larger vessels. Yet even here

there was no relief: for as each tributary stream ingurgitated its protoplasmic horde, these too became stuffed to suffocation; so that, though every corpuscle strove onward with all his strength, the jammed and stifled cell mass could scarce be seen to move. Here and there bands of armed Phagocytes, impatient of delay, tried to cut themselves a passage through the helpless huddled mass of Lymphocytes and Platelets: but they succeeded only in walling themselves up with impenetrable mounds of slaughtered carcases. Still more frightful scenes occurred when two mobs, travelling by anastomosing vessels, met each other head to head: for while those in front fought in grim despair for possession of the road until it was totally blocked and thrombosed with their bodies, the cells behind, still harried by fear, pressed onward as vigorously as ever, to the great discomfiture of the dense crowds packed between, who, thus driven by an irresistible force against an impenetrable obstacle, perished in millions.

Thus was the Manager's blood very literally curdled. . . .

This same civilized delight with inventiveness and with form is also what makes the volume a loose burlesque of the saga. The volume starts with the Pillow-Chat of Goshawk and Guzzelinda, as, of course, The Tain starts with the pillow talk of Ailill and Medb. And the following memorable passage is a parody of the saga hero's rage:

Each hair of his head stood on end, with a drop of blood at its tip. One of his eyes started forth a hand's breadth out of its socket, and the other was sucked down into the depths of his breast. His whole body was contorted. His ribs parted asunder, so that there was room for a man's foot between them; his calves and his buttocks came round to the front of his body. At the same time the hero-light shone around his head, and the Bocanachs and Bananachs and the Witches of the Valley raised a shout around him.

Indeed, the problem in describing this book is that

it has such a plenitude of invention and so few aridities that one almost does an injustice by choosing. There is an inane and yet fearfully pertinent war between the Wolfians and the Lambians, which is nicely reminiscent of Swift's war between the Big-Endians and the Little-Endians. There is the droll chapter describing the Shaw Centenary, at which GBS is admired for his "delightful human creations, untroubled by the cloven hoof of the propagandist." But those, of course, were the good old days of the theatre before the present morbid tendency to choose unpleasant subjects, when "the kindly human sentiment of Ibsen and the innocent gaiety of Shaw gave clean healthy entertainment to young and old." There is also a brilliant chapter which broadly parodies a contemporary newspaper, and includes news stories, leading articles, sports reports, book reviews, gossip about celebrities, and even advertisements. Among the advertisements, for instance, one finds:

LIMELIGHT CINEMA
All This Week
RODERICK REDLIP and BETTY BRIGHTEYE
in
TAVY'S BROKEN HEART
Adapted from Shaw's touching romance
Man and Superman.

Or, in the Houses to Let section of the Classified advertisements:

A five-roomed house to let. South suburbs. Moderate rent. No children. . . .

Delightful house. Five miles from city. Six bed, four reception rooms. Billiard room, conservatory, stables,

garage, kennels, garden and kitchen garden. No children.
Gate lodge to let. Five rooms. No dogs, no poultry, no children. Suit married couple. . . .
Pigstye to let. 10s. weekly. Suit large family.

Or, in a news story:

> A murder of a peculiarly dastardly character was perpetrated to-day by tribesmen in the neighbourhood of Jhamjhar, Jungulay. The victim was Lieut. Derek Blacktan, an officer in King Goshawk's Air Force stationed at Brahmbuhl Jhelli. Entirely unarmed save for a loaded revolver, he happened to be strolling in the vicinity of Jhamjhar, when he was set upon by three natives and beaten to death. The village had been bombed from the air a few days before, and it is believed that the assassination was an act of vengeance. Reprisals are already in preparation.

In sum, this is a brilliant, original and inordinately quotable satire, whose ferocity is ever leavened with whimsy, and whose rage is ever controlled by art.

In its sequel, *The Spacious Adventures of the Man in the Street,* O'Duffy presents a more formally organized satire than he had in *King Goshawk.* His device is the same as Swift's in *Gulliver's Travels:* he introduces a man from our society into an alien society, and uses the follies and good sense of the alien society to criticize by implication the follies and bad sense of our own.

His Gulliver is Aloysius O'Kennedy, whose body the old Philosopher had rented for the use of Cuchulain during his visit to earth. While Cuchulain was inhabiting O'Kennedy's body (and also stretching it out of shape), O'Kennedy's spirit sped into outer space and eventually wound up on the planet of Rathé, where he took on the body of a recently executed Rathean,

Ydenneko. Rathé, of course, is an anagram for earth, and that portion of Rathé where O'Kennedy spends most of his time is a kind of semi-Utopia, which lacks many of the social follies of Earth, but which has a few analagous follies of its own.

For instance, the Ratheans do not eat promiscuously as we do on Earth; they are instead "monophagous," and O'Kennedy soon learns that is is very bad form—vulgar, if not indeed obscene—to say that he is hungry or to ask for something to eat. The Ratheans do not totally abstain from food, however, for they choose, not by its taste but by its smell and appearance, one fruit to which they remain wedded for life. They may possibly find out later, after having tasted the fruit, that it does not agree with them, but they are still indissolubly wedded to it. There are some few illicit cafes, at which suspicious looking food can be illegally purchased, and O'Kennedy remarks, "From the number of these houses and from the prominence given in jest, song, and story to the theme of dietetic infidelity, I imagine that disobedience to the law must be very common indeed. . . ." O'Kennedy also notes that the Ratheans are obsessed with the subject of food; they never crudely mention the word "hunger," but the word "taste" is never out of their mouths. Taste "is universally agreed to be the dominant impulse of human nature. It is the noblest of all sentiments. It is fixed, unchanging, immortal. It is the noblest of all sentiments. It is the mainspring of man's highest activities. Its gratification is the supreme joy, and sufficient reward for all endeavours. The world and all else are well lost for Taste." The parallel, of course, to the attitudes of our society about marriage, sex and love is beautifully telling, and O'Duffy works the parallelism out with a multitude of deftly chosen details.

The religion of the Ratheans is another intricately extended parallel. The Ratheans worship not God but the Devil. This would seem to make for a particularly vicious society, but in fact the Ratheans, like the people of earth, give only lip service to their Deity. The ordinary transactions of their social life are conducted with a quite irreligious virtue, even though when they approach death they might attempt to make some minimal amends by whipping a child or killing a flower. The chief prophet of the Rathean religion was Procrustes, and the religion is named Procrusteanity. The Rathean religion is upheld not by theologians, philosophers and poets, but by a College of Scientists whose hidebound and reactionary inanities are a constant deterrent to the brilliant advances of civilization discovered by the philosophers and poets. The wealth of circumstantial detail which O'Duffy brings to this conception is a mordantly exact gloss upon some central, deeply ingrained biases of our own society.

Furthermore, the parallel is cleverly extended to include detailed discussions of Rathean government, economics, education and even letters. One of their notable novelists, for instance, is named Sneckid, and one of their notable playwrights is Nesbi, whose play *Phantoms* is an outspoken discussion of the controversial theme of gluttony and how its disastrous consequences can be inherited even by the second generation.

This portion of the book is quite the longest and also possibly the finest thing that O'Duffy ever wrote. His ingenuity is unflagging, his satire is consistently adroit, and his prose often rises from a basic ease to memorably eloquent statements such as this remark of a Rathean statesman to O'Kennedy: "Do you think life has no greater purpose than to develop an omnivorous belly served by an omnirapient claw?"

In *The Wasted Island,* the education of Bernard Lascelles was related by a series of lengthy, meaty and heated conversations, and much of O'Kennedy's education in this section of the book is the same Gulliver-King of Brobdingnag sort of thing. Although he is overtly and lengthily dealing with ideas, O'Duffy avoids dullness by the stupidity and illogic of O'Kennedy. This is a canny satiric device which was often used by Shaw in the many pupil-teacher dialogues in his plays. O'Duffy's discussions are usually long, but because they are such a central part of his strategy here is a portion of a typical one:

> I had been paying a round of calls with my Lady, and as we left the last house on our list she happened to mention that the gentleman who lived there was a remarkably brilliant plumber. I said 'O!' having never known an earthly plumber, however brilliant, to be housed so elegantly. Then, by questioning my Lady, I learned that the other people we had visited were a railway-director, a University professor, and a bricklayer: whereupon I remarked that it was curious that they should all have such similar houses.
>
> 'Why?' asked her Ladyship. The Ratheans were like a lot of babies with their whys.
>
> 'O, well, because—' I began and floundered hopelessly in the bog of their lingo. 'In our world' I managed at last 'a plumber would live in a house of three rooms, and a railway-director in one of thirty.'
>
> 'Indeed?' said her Ladyship. 'Are your railway-directors so prolific?'
>
> 'O no' I said. 'If it comes to that it's the plumbers that produce the families. But railway-directors are—oh,

bother this language of yours—they're—well—more high-up and important sort of people than plumbers.'

'Are they?' said her Ladyship, looking puzzled.

'Well, aren't they?' I answered.

'I don't know what you mean' said her Ladyship stupidly. 'Surely all people are equally important?'

'I suppose they are here' I said. 'But on Earth a railway director is thought more highly of.'

'So is he here' said her Ladyship. 'He has a more difficult task, which develops a more highly-evolved brain, than a plumber. But what has that to do with the size of their houses?'

'Well' I said, 'we think that a man in a highly specialized job ought to have rather better accommodations than an ordinary manual worker.'

'I see' said her Ladyship brightly. 'So you fix the size of a person's house according to his value to the community?'

'That's about it' I said.

'What unpractical dreamers you must be' smiled her Ladyship. 'Idealists, of course, I admit, but how utterly unpractical! How can you possibly estimate with any sort of accuracy the comparative values of each and every trade? And after that, how are you to proportion the houses? Why, my dear boy'—with an impatient shrug of the shoulders—'the whole thing is fantastically Utopian and impossible. . . .'

As in *Gulliver's Travels*, the remainder of the book is not quite on the same high level. The people in O'Duffy's Isles of the Blest suffer from some of the same difficulties as do Swift's horses and Shaw's He-Ancients and She-Ancients. The problem of the Utopian writer is always to find a persuasive objectification of a virtuous society. It is a difficult problem because the inhabitants of Utopias tend to be contemplative, unmaterialistic, almost mystic. Like Swift's Utopia and like Bernard Shaw's, O'Duffy's is the simplest primitive gathering of beings. His people resemble Shaw's in that they are born with most of their powers, and in a very few years they pass through the necessity for ordinary human emotions and actions, such as the childish desire to create a work of art or to make love. Soon they sink more and more into contemplation and prayer. They are not so forbidding looking as Shaw's bald and sexless Utopians, and certainly not so ungainly as Swift's horses. Rather, they are extraordinarily tall and handsome, and differ from ordinary beings only in that they have a cloak-like membrane falling from their shoulders, which they use to fly. When the people mature, these membranes atrophy.

This section of the book does contain one lively episode in which a Utopian, who is fully grown although not quite three years old, attempts to teach O'Kennedy how to fly. However, O'Duffy no more than his illustrious predecessors has solved the problem of writing about Utopia, and this short section is the weakest in the book.

In the third section, O'Duffy and an exiled Rathean journey to the dark side of the planet, and in this dark side O'Duffy portrays his Hell. His Hell is, of course, an exaggerated view of the excesses of modern capitalistic society in the jazz age. Although not without its powerful moments, the satire in general here is much broader, even for O'Duffy, and more overt than that of the main section of the book. The best moments are not the frenetic drinking and dancing in the night club, but the satire of the sycophantic lower classes. The workers are ghastly dwarfs who have allowed their tibias to be cut out in infancy in order that they may fit into their houses. The houses are all quite small because there is not enough material to build them larger, or at least it would be more effort than it is worth. To avoid various other social ills, the workers have had their noses and ears cropped, and there is, when O'Kennedy arrives, a movement to shorten their necks. This seems in the retelling a crude conception, but O'Duffy's circumstantial details are as happily chosen as those in Swift's own modest proposal. O'Duffy's apologists for short necks speak in exactly the same plausible phrases and with the same reasonable arguments as do apologists for any intolerable but convenient social evil: "Ah, my young friend, if only you knew the conditions under which these miserable people lived before this great reform was introduced, you would change your opinion. I am old enough to remember the time when the operation was still voluntary, and I do assure you that the conditions were too shocking for words. . . ."

The sycophantic lower-middle class, or silent majority, is satirized by the dog society. The dogs have been injected with some modicum of human brains, and they slavishly imitate the humans by shaving their faces and forepaws, and by cultivating the second-hand vices of the rich.

Despite many good touches, this section is hardly as satirically fine as the long section which begins the book, but it is considerably redeemed by action. The journey to the dark lands is a harrowing bit of pre-Tolkien, and the section is concluded by O'Kennedy leading in most mounmental confusion an army to attack Rathé.

The final section of the book, after O'Kennedy's execution by the Ratheans, shows his disembodied spirit in space confronting various gods—Moloch; Zeus; Jehovah with a lollipop and a thunderbolt; Reason, a "hard-faced woman in a red cap," with a hypodermic syringe in one hand and "a flayed dog writhing beneath her feet"; a hermaphroditic god of Love and Beauty who remarks that "There is no fact so unpleasant that we cannot shut our eyes to it." And finally, briefly, O'Kennedy encounters the Devil who asserts he is greater than any of the five gods O'Kennedy has created. "I am the unimaginable and the undeniable. I am Darkness. I am the enemy of the gods. I am he that has marred all the gods of your making. I stand between you and the god that is to be." And after this précis of Shavian Creative Evolution, O'Kennedy is returned to earth, to the body that Cuchulain had wrenched out of shape and left on the ash heap.

O'Kennedy is as much Man as was Gulliver, and O'Duffy's attitude toward him is precisely and terrifically Swiftean. The King of Brobdingnag was no grimmer toward Gulliver than is O'Kennedy's judge toward him at his trial:

> It was doubtful, he said, whether the race to which the Prisoner belonged should be classed as a very low type of man or a rather high type of ape. They [the Judges] had not allowed themselves to be influenced by what they had learnt of the physical aspect of the creatures, though the general conformation of the head, particularly in the opthalmic region, was undoubtedly simian. Their researches had been mainly conducted into our mental and physiological characteristics; and on this basis the evidence was uncertain, confused, and contradictory. Our quarrelsomeness, ferocity, vindictiveness, and general love of mischief were markedly simian indications, as were our acquisitiveness, our mania for collecting useless things, our vanity, our addiction to meaningless chatter, our gluttony, and our insatiable sexuality, which was tempered only by irrational taboos. On the other hand, it was evident that we had some

rudimentary reasoning powers, of which, however, we made very little use, and that we could both speak and write, and had even some primitive artistic instincts. Again, traces of elementary religious ideas were obviously discernible in our composition, though it was doubtful if we had any deeper ethical conception than the animal notion of reward and punishment. The examiners, therefore, begged to report that they were unable, in the time at their disposal, to come to any definite conclusion as to whether the race in question were human or not; but they considered that it was sufficiently probable to justify the court in giving the prisoner the benefit of the doubt.

This volume is a brilliant sequel to *King Goshawk and the Birds*. It probably even betters the original. Unfortunately, it also set an enormously high standard, and the concluding volume of the trilogy rarely approaches its excellence.

IV

There was an interval of several years between *The Spacious Adventures of the Man in the Street* and the final volume of the trilogy, *Asses in Clover*. In those years, O'Duffy published some quickly written detective thrillers, and three different versions of a book on economics.

O'Duffy's three potboilers are his poorest work. They include *The Bird Cage, The Secret Enemy,* and *Heart of a Girl.* Each was written in about three months' time, and each is part thriller and part detective story. In *The Bird Cage,* there is not one, but a number of detectives. The style is lucid, even though it has a few turgid, probably hastily written passages. It contains a couple of small sermons on economics which are rather gratuitously intruded. There is a bit of satire, although it is rather too broad for its context. There is nothing particularly in either the plot or the characterization to make one remember it a month after one has read it.

The Secret Enemy, however, does have some minor merits as well as some rather typical faults. Among the faults, the chief is that the culprit is revealed quite a way before the book is over, and so the novel is not so much a whodunnit as a whatwasit. Neither of the book's two detectives manages to unravel what exactly was the nature of the crime that had been committed. It is only the villain's confession that reveals the crime was not murder but suicide which he had arranged to look like murder. At times, it seems almost as if O'Duffy were scarcely concealing his contempt for his form. The names of some of his characters are a case in point—particularly the languid young rotter with the impossible name of Sydney Flowerdew.

Among the book's merits are a locked-room problem worked out with some ingenuity, and an interesting handling of the love story which, predictably for O'Duffy, does not end romantically but realistically. The heroine, though appealing, is a little too short, a little too stocky, eats a few too many sweets, and has certain intellectual limitations. The young hero, while infatuated for a time, has finally some moments of hideous clarity in which he recoils from the match in horror.

Other than this, the characterization ranges from the dully adequate to the skimpy. There are a few rather broad touches of satire about modern poetry or modern capitalism, but, although it is somewhat better than *The Bird Cage, The Secret Enemy* contains only hints of O'Duffy's real merits and preoccupations.

Heart of a Girl is more thriller than mystery. The story has a typical O'Duffian love triangle. There is the beautiful, vapid girl; there is the plain and brilliant girl who is also the chief detective; and in the center there is the rather thick-witted narrator-hero. There is also a Jeeves character in the hero's valet. The whole business is readable, but more far-fetched than the earlier thrillers. The heroine, for instance, is so brilliant that Scotland Yard brings her in as unofficial consultant, and she even once pops up at a cabinet meeting and delivers herself of a few scathing remarks about capitalism.

At one point in the book, O'Duffy describes American detective fiction:

> The machine-made villainy, the complete absence of character in the people, the laboriously manufactured 'thrills', the cheap smartness of the writing, the dreary cliches when the supply of this ran short, were such a bore that over and over again I found myself dropping asleep.

This is certainly a fair enough criticism, but O'Duffy's own detective fiction did not rise notably above it. Except for some small touches of real characterization in *The Secret Enemy* and *Heart of a Girl,* and for a few pages of not really integrated satire on economics, he gave little to these quickly written books to make them notable. Undoubtedly they brought in a little money, which was no doubt exactly what they were supposed to do, but there would be no point whatsoever in their being reissued.

I am quite totally unqualified to discuss O'Duffy's *Life and Money*. Nevertheless, it stands in the same relation to his creative work as Bernard Shaw's *The Intelligent Woman's Guide to Socialism and Capitalism* does to his plays. Indeed, if anything, *Life and Money* is more important for an understanding of O'Duffy's last work than *The Intelligent Woman's Guide* is for an understanding of Shaw.

O'Duffy's book came out originally in 1932 and

quickly went into two revised editions. It was an analysis of the causes for the Depression, and an indictment of the economic system which had so spectacularly broken down in 1929. More important, if undoubtedly less sound, was O'Duffy's remedy, a kind of modified social-capitalism whose chief feature was its money reform—in other words, a Social Credit scheme.

In the most general sense, O'Duffy's view is that:

> The economic troubles of the world are occasioned by the fact that a monetary system which originated at a time when the demand for goods was greater than the supply, and when competition between man and man was inevitable, is still in use at a time when the supply of goods is greater than the demand, and competition is giving place to co-operation.

The monetary system of the world caused in O'Duffy's time the anomaly of millions of people starving in the midst of plenty. He wrote:

> Modern industry is so well equipped and organized that it can produce enough goods to satisfy everybody's wants without calling on everybody to work. But in spite of this, society insists that no individual shall take a share of the product unless he works. In consequence, the goods which an unemployed man would consume are presently left unproduced, with the result that those who would have made them are unemployed in their turn, and a fresh shrinkage of production follows, leading to more unemployment, and so on *ad infinitum*.

According to O'Duffy, the two most usual economic remedies are Sisyphism and Procrusteanism. The sterile labors of Sisyphus are for O'Duffy "an excellent symbol for the policy of 'making work' instead of distributing the product." Following Frederic Bastiat, a nineteenth-century French economist, O'Duffy outlines Sisyphist reasoning as follows: Industry is an effort followed by a result; the result is wealth or prosperity; and hence it would seem to follow that the greater the industry the greater the wealth. Consequently, the Sisyphist, when faced by some economic catastrophe, attempts to remedy it not by a distribution of goods, but by the creation of work. This was the highly inadequate remedy of the British government during the Great Famine in Ireland in the nineteenth century. O'Duffy notes that De Valera's statement that Ireland had been well served by its Civil War because repairing the damage would cause employment, was nothing but Sisyphism. Or the French Minister who opposed the cultivation of sugar beets on the grounds that it required little land, labor and capital to provide a large amount of sugar, was nothing but a Sisyphist. Or the W. P. A. in the United States during the Depression was nothing, in O'Duffy's view, but a Sisyphist makeshift.

According to O'Duffy, "the way to prosperity is to increase the proportion which result bears to effort: to get the maximum result from the minimum of effort." In his view, the problem in a time of plenty is not to create artificial employment, but properly to distribute goods and leisure.

A second usual economic remedy O'Duffy calls Procrusteanism, and the Procrustean remedy is to fit the society to the economic muddle. The most usual methods advanced to do this are emigration and birth control. The great hue and cry today about overpopulation and the immediate necessity for birth control over the world would be regarded by O'Duffy as rampant Procrusteanism and an admission that the economic system is unable to function efficiently. The recent demands of Mr. Enoch Powell in England, that immigration to England by citizens from other of the Commonwealth nations should be immediately curtailed, and that the two million Irishmen working in England should be immediately deported, are Procrustean solutions to the country's economic problems.

O'Duffy's solution, which he works out in ingenious detail, is a form of Social Credit. We have allowed, he says, the banker to treat credit as his own private property:

> We have allowed him to grant or withold the use of it at his own discretion, to charge us interest on it while it is lent to us, and to withdraw it at his pleasure to our own prejudice. The foundation stone of the new system, therefore, must be the restoration of this credit-power to its rightful owners, the people, and its administration by a national authority in the people's interest.

He then proposes that, instead of issuing a currency based on gold, that a new currency should be issued annually based on consumable goods, under a guarantee of cancellation with the consumption of the goods. Or, as he sums the argument up:

1. That money shall be valueless, a mere ticket for the exchange of goods.

2. That the issue and control of money shall be in the hands of a national authority responsible to the people.

3. That the amount of money issued in any particular period shall be equal to the collective prices of the goods available in the same period.

4. That goods shall be sold at their true economic price, calculated scientifically.

5. That a National Industrial Dividend shall be paid

to every citizen without conditions as to work.

6. That new capital developments shall be financed out of new credits created for the purpose instead of out of savings.

Then in great detail, he outlines a plan for the administration of the scheme. This resumé is, of course, a considerable simplification of the bare outlines of O'Duffy's scheme. However, I am sure that the perusal of the scheme in all of its rather persuasive detail would still undoubtedly lead one to conclude that this is only the visionary Utopia of yet another crank. Indeed, Bernard Shaw in *Everybody's Political What's What* takes the following caustic view toward the various schemes of Social Credit:

> Finance and money are much more puzzling than direct commercial profiteering for one's own hand with one's own little capital. They produce crazy schemes to which the Everyman family lends a greedy ear, as they all promise plenty of money for nothing. The Currency Crank is a nuisance in every movement for social reform; and the apostles of Social Credit once actually persuaded a Canadian legislature to budget on its imaginary riches. They are supported by the mystery of banking, which seems to create millions of money out of nothing, and by the fact, of which everyone has daily experience, that scraps of paper are accepted in discharge of debts of thousands of golden ponnds. In these phenomena there is much more substantial evidence for the existence of the philosopher's stone, with its power of transmuting base metals into precious ones, than the old alchemists were ever able to produce. We may cease to believe in the philosopher's stone, and be convinced by the experience of the Alberta exchequer that there is something wrong with Social Credit; but as long as banking remains a private business, and rich people enjoy enormous unearned incomes without lifting their little fingers to earn it, there will be crazy schemes in the air under one name or another; and the Everyman

> family will run after them just as they ran after the South Sea Bubble.

Shaw's conclusion is just, inasmuch as it is inconceivable that a scheme like O'Duffy's would be implemented anywhere in the foreseeable future. In the hysteria that followed the Crash of 1929, however, when it was perfectly obvious to everyone that the economic system was most lamentably inadequate, his scheme probably appeared to large numbers of the Everyman family as worth some consideration. At any rate, his book very quickly went into three editions. In the economic recovery which was largely impelled by the vast creation of work necessitated by a World War, schemes such as O'Duffy's were relegated to the dusty back shelves of libraries.

Yet perhaps one should not dismiss this volume quite so easily, for the soundness of its indictment may certainly still be seen in the patchwork Socialism of the great nations in the post-war world. Even such an economically reactionary country as Ireland has found it absolutely necessary to provide an imposing array of doles, welfare services, and state control of various key industries. This worldwide fact, plus the equally apparent floundering of the economy of the great nations, would indicate to this writer's admittedly ignorant view of the situation that a scheme like O'Duffy's may be thoroughly impractical but nevertheless right. Or at least more right than the various economic bandaids that have been applied to a cancerous economy in the postwar world.

Asses in Clover is the final volume in the Cuanduine

trilogy. It takes up again the story of Cuanduine and his battles against the modern economic system, as personified by King Goshawk and his comic-strip colleagues. As a story, this last book is much more rambling and ineffectual than was either *King Goshawk and the Birds* or *The Spacious Adventures of the Man in the Street.* The reason is largely that O'Duffy was, during much of the writing, suffering acute physical pain, and it is remarkable that he was able to complete the book at all.

Its plot begins with a council of state between Goshawk and his liege kings, then diverges to chart at length the adventures of a new character, Mac ui Rudai, who is a kind of hyper-typical man on the street, and then after 160 pages or so returns leisurely to the original story of the birds. One of the birds has escaped from Queen Gusselinda's aviary and taken refuge in Ireland, where the natives refuse to give him up. Goshawk and his men mount a massive air attack upon Ireland, intending to devastate the country with bombs and poison gas. Cuanduine goes to Ireland, constructs a great airplane, and then in an excellently conceived battle scene destroys Goshawk's airforce. He next attacks Goshawk's castle, and although Goshawk is destroyed, his economic adviser, Mr. Slawmy Cander who is the real power in the world, is spared. Because Cander's power is so pervasive, Cuanduine finds it impossible to liberate the birds. So, giving up his attempt to reform the world, he returns to his wife, only to discover that his children have in his absence become creatures of the modern world. Quite thoroughly disgusted, Cuanduine and his wife fly away from the earth, never to be seen again.

There yet remain six chapters in the book, which tell

what happened to the earth after the failure of Cuanduine. According to O'Duffy's reading of contemporary economics, the ironic central fallacy is that the capitalist state produces goods which the workers who produce them cannot afford to buy. Therefore, at the suggestion of O'Kennedy, who has returned from his travels on Rathé, an expedition is launched to the moon to open up a new market among its inhabitants. This works excellently for a while, but then:

> After a time, indeed, the stream of goods began to diminish, because the imports of Selenite material [from the moon] could not keep pace with it. Unemployment at once began to rear its unwelcome head again on earth; but Mr. Cander was not to be defeated so easily. He arranged that in future the surplus profits should be invested in new enterprises on the spot: in other words, terrestrial-owned industries were to be started on lunar territory. This solved the difficulty for a time, giving much-needed employment to the 'heavy' industries; but after a while the competition of the lunar factories began to be felt, prices fell, and many terrestrial businesses were ruined. Only one course now remained: to conquer the Moon, and bring it within the ambit of the Earth's financial system. As the Economists put it, the economic problem was One Big Two-World Problem which could not be solved on narrow one-world lines.

The great powers of the earth—the British, the Americans, and the Japanese—all claim the moon as their rightful province and launch expeditions to subdue it. On the moon, however, the three expeditions spend most of their time destroying each other, and the remainder of the earth armies is easily repulsed by the Selenites. Then the great powers of the earth combine in several joint expeditions to subdue the moon, but when these too are easily repulsed all hope is given up for the project.

The effect on the Earth was immediate and tragic. Deprived of the only available market, industry after industry went smash, and the world sank into the blackest trade depression it had ever known.

This depression was followed by a great war which destroyed most of the civilized world and reduced the few remaining inhabitants to a primitive pastoral existence. In a few more years, the society of men has been succeeded by a society of rabbits, and in the last chapter two of the Gods "observed a dim star among the drifting millions flash suddenly, and go out." One of the Gods muses that, "There ends another of my experiments."

And the second God inquires, "A successful one?"

"Nay, a miserable failure, though at one time it gave good promise. That star gave birth to a number of planets, on one of which I evolved, after much thought and toil, a strange creature called Man. At first he was truly interesting, but he reached his zenith too quickly, and then rapidly declined. During his last few hundred years, when he was already far gone in decay, he achieved a mastery of natural forces that was marvelous in a race so stupid, but his wickedness and folly were such that it did him more harm than good. In the end I superseded him by a somewhat lower creature called rabbit; but this had no great potentialities either for good or evil, and so nothing came of it. A few million years ago the planet fell back into its parent sun, which has now itself come to an end."

"Did these Men that you have mentioned achieve nothing of lasting worth?" asked the other God.

"Almost nothing," replied the first. "A few of them did occasionally show some glimmerings of divine wisdom, to which their fellows paid no heed. That, and some trifles of tolerable music, is their only memorial. If you listen you may catch some echo of the latter still moving among the spheres."

The Gods were silent; and the ghost of the Ninth Symphony came stealing through the ether.

This is an effectively wry conclusion to a highly talented writer's major work, a trilogy that could have been one of the great satiric works of its time. There are several major flaws in the trilogy, and they are most apparent in this final volume. The book was written when the world was in the throes of a great economic depression, and the intensity of O'Duffy's feelings about the Depression keeps breaking out into overt statement. Particularly in the early portion of the book does this preaching occur. There, the fable of Mac ui Rudai is particularly slack and unimpressive. Only sporadically in *Asses in Clover* did O'Duffy effectively objectify his point.

This impatience with his fable often leads O'Duffy into satire that is superficial and slapdash. His America, for instance, hangs between the America of Bertold Brecht and the America of Al Capp. His captains of industry with their absurd names sometimes have the effectiveness of Brecht's similar device in such plays as *St. Joan of the Stockyards,* a hideous fantasy whose idiotically unfair exaggerations nevertheless suggest a grotesquely distorted version of the truth, and perhaps even suggest that the truth itself partakes of some of that distortion. But sometimes the mere names, when little else is done with them—names such as "Scab" Slughorn the Crime King, Gurgleheim the Liquor King, and Pulpenbaum the Paper King—are little more than the puerile satiric shortcuts of *L'il Abner.* Capp's calling a senator, for instance, Jack S. Phogbound is simply exaggerated without being clever, and so his satire is thin stuff indeed. The same fault is too often evident in O'Duffy.

The seriousness of the message has so taken over in *Asses in Clover* that the book breaks into several not too closely connected segments, and there is to the inventiveness no consistency. Only at intervals, such as the battle in the air and the story of the imperturbably unproductive Selenites, does the quality of the invention rise to the level of the previous two volumes. In O'Duffy's defense, I suppose it could be said that the importance of the subject matter simply overwhelmed him. As often happened with D. H. Lawrence and even occasionally with Shaw, the preacher overcame the artist.

In several portions of the book, the satire is simply too blatant to be effective. When O'Duffy turns his criticism to the jazz age, as he had toward the end also of *The Spacious Adventures of the Man in the Street,* he usually becomes merely crude and obvious. For instance:

> My dear, how perfectly devastating! Quite. Quite. No, he wasn't *quite* quite, you see. I believe shoulders are coming in again in the autumn. What a bore! Quite. My dear, her hat was quite too erroneous. Let me introduce you two. How're you, darling? Put it there, old top. The fellow is perfectly *eocene*—he actually believes in things. Yes, I shall probably remarry Bert if he's keen, but I'd just as soon go on living with him as we are now. Quite too absolutely downcasting. Quite. On the whole I rather enjoyed the war: it began to be a bore towards the end, but the first few years were quite jolly. . . .

Or in the same chapter his parodies of popular songs are equally poor:

Blue cabbages are blooming down in Bluelick,
In Kentucky.
Ain't that lucky?
So jangle all your bangles and we'll splash the ole spondulicks
In the lil home town that I was born in.
Then we'll bang the ole pianna
By the dusky Susquehanna,
Lil yaller-faced baby o' mine!
I wanna say me cutie
Has gotta bitta beauty
Whoop-ya! Whoop-ya! Whoop!
An' we gonna hang our washin' in de mornin'
On de Mason-Dixon Line.

All this smacks too much of the writer who is tired and ill.

There are still patches of pure delight. For instance, there is the discussion between the two parties in Ireland, the Trimmers and the Slashers, who disagree about the best way to combat Goshawk's Air Force:

> At first the Trimmers had been content to describe the Slashers as rash and imprudent, and the Slashers to call the Trimmers over-cautious and deficient in enterprise. But before long they took to more vigorous language, inveighing against each other in a degringolade of courtesy after this fashion:

Trimmers:	Slashers:
Over-confident enthusiasts	Faint-hearted compromisers
Audacious gamblers	Timid ineffectives
Reckless hot-heads	Spiritless slackers
Foolhardy jingoes	Pusillanimous defeatists
Brawling flag-wavers	Trembling white-flaggers
Mad swashbucklers	Frightened poltroons
Swashbuckling idiots	Skulking runaways
Truculent fools	Lily-livered cowards
Fire-eating nincompoops	Dirt-eating cravens
Senseless fanatics	Soulless dastards
Insensate furies	Worthless degenerates

This catalogue continues through, on the one side, "Raving maniacs, Criminal lunatics, Thoroughpaced scoundrels, detestable ruffians, Bloody-minded butchers, Sanguinary cut-throats, Diabolical murderers, Brutal Savages, Inhuman Monsters, Incarnate fiends and Spawn of Satan," and, on the other side, "Cringing slaves, Cowering lick-spittles, Abject kiss-the-rods, Sneaking rotters, Fawning puppets, Contemptible wretches, Grovelling serfs, Snivelling curs, Stinking reptiles, Loathsome skunks, and Scum of the Earth," and then magnificently culminates in their mutual epithets of:

> Creatures unworthy of the name of Irishmen
> Scurrilous calumniators
> Foulmouthed slanderers
> Unscrupulous liars
> Traitors!

This has a fine Rabelaisian gusto to it, but there are few such heady passages in *Asses in Clover,* which must finally be called a pedestrian conclusion to one of the most ambitious and brilliant works penned by an Irishman in the twentieth century.

O'Duffy is difficult to sum up. The circumstances of his life were against him, and he had no opportunity, or perhaps inclination, to develop in a straight line. His penchant for light verse he did toy with for most of his career, and most of his books have a few limericks or a bit of doggerel somewhere in them. However, he was no W. S. Gilbert and not even an Ogden Nash, and among his own countrymen Susan L. Mitchell beats him hands down. His plays are more than competent, and the dramatic form which he also used for a chapter in *Printer's Errors* and a chapter in *King Goshawk* indicates that he could well have become a significant dramatist. Indeed, P. S. O'Hegarty seems to think of him primarily as a dramatist. His *Wasted Island,* for all of its occasional crudities of style, is an engrossing, ambitious, and impressive book. Had he continued to write in this vein of fictionalized intellectual history, Irish literature would have been significantly enriched, as would it also had he continued his historical fiction which he began so promisingly in *The Lion and the Fox.* In fact, had he continued even to write in the vein of light comic fiction, which he so successfully essayed in *Printer's Errors* and *Miss Rudd and Some Lovers,* he would ultimately, I feel certain, have created an audience. His thrillers are best forgotten, and probably so also is his book on economics which has its primary interest as an overt statement of the attitudes impelling the Cuanduine trilogy. That trilogy had he been able to conclude it in the same dazzling manner in which he had written the first two volumes would have been an unforgettably imposing masterpiece. However, worries and ill health intervened, and the final volume, despite flashes of brilliance, has its dreary longeurs.

Yet despite his hectic and diverse and spotty writing career, O'Duffy had his memorable accomplishments, and this tone of rather severe reservation really only implies a regret that his splendid accomplishments were not so great as his remarkable potentialities.

Bibliography

I. *Principal Works*

The Walls of Athens: A Comedy in Allegory. Dublin: The Irish Review, 1914.

A Lay of the Liffey, and Other Verses. Dublin: The Candle Press, 1918.

Bricriu's Feast: A Comedy in Three Acts, with an Epilogue. Dublin: Martin Lester, Ltd., [1919?].

The Wasted Island. Dublin: Martin Lester, Ltd., [1919]; rev. ed., London: Macmillan, 1929.

A College Chorus: A Collection of Humorous Verses by Students of University College, Dublin, from the pages of "St. Stephen's" and "The National Student," ed. by Eimar O'Duffy. Dublin: Martin Lester, Ltd., n. d.

Printer's Errors. Dublin: Martin Lester, Ltd., 1922; London: Leonard Parsons, Ltd., [1922].

The Lion and the Fox. Dublin: Martin Lester, Ltd., [1922].

Miss Rudd and some Lovers. Dublin: The Talbot Press, 1923.

King Goshawk and the Birds. London: Macmillan, 1926.

The Spacious Adventures of the Man in the Street.

London: Macmillan, 1928.

Life and Money. London and New York: Putnam's, 1932; 2nd ed., revised and enlarged, 1933; 3rd ed., revised, 1935.

The Bird Cage: A Mystery Novel. London: Geoffrey Bles, 1932.

The Secret Enemy: A Mystery Novel. London: Geoffrey Bles, 1932.

Asses in Clover. London: Putnam's, 1933.

Consumer Credit: A Pamphlet. London: The Prosperity League, 1934.

Heart of a Girl: A Mystery Novel. London: Geoffrey Bles, [1935].

II. *Works about O'Duffy*

Other than a handful of not particularly perceptive book reviews, there has been very little written about O'Duffy. Vivian Mercier's introductory article, "The Satires of Eimar O'Duffy" in *The Bell,* XII (July 1946), pp. 325–336, should be consulted; and Mercier has also a short discussion of *King Goshawk and the Birds* and *Asses in Clover* in *The Irish Comic Tradition* (Oxford: Oxford University Press, 1962). See pp. 205–207. There are a number of scattered remarks in Benedict Kiely's excellent study *Modern Irish Fiction—A Critique* (Dublin: Golden Eagle Books, Ltd., 1950), but Kiely to my mind does O'Duffy considerably less than justice, and indeed does not mention some of his best work. I have made some use of P. S. O'Hegarty's short obituary in *The Dublin Magazine,* X, New Series (July–September 1935). See p. 92. I have also referred to the obituary notices in several Dublin newspapers. Among the Bulmer Hobson papers contained in the National Library of Ireland, I have found several

O'Duffy letters, and I have also used several of Hobson's typescript accounts of the Irish Volunteers, as well as J. J. O'Connell's manuscript *History of the Irish Volunteers.* I have found occasional references to O'Duffy in such volumes as *The Irish Volunteers, 1913–1915,* ed. F. X. Martin, O. S. A. (Dublin: James Duffy & Co., Ltd., 1963) ; Charles Duff's *Six Days to Shake an Empire* (London: J. M. Dent & Sons, Ltd., 1966) ; and the *Memoirs of Desmond Fitzgerald* (London: Routledge & Kegan Paul, 1968) . However, none of these latter sources has said very much.